James J. Andrews

THE HISTORIC GENERAL

A Thrilling Episode
of the Civil War

by
Randell W. McBryde

THE CONFEDERATE
REPRINT COMPANY
☆   ☆   ☆   ☆
WWW.CONFEDERATEREPRINT.COM

The Historic General:
A Thrilling Episode of the Civil War
by Randell W. McBryde

Originally Published in 1904
by MacGowan & Cooke Co.
Chattanooga, Tennessee

Reprint Edition © 2016
The Confederate Reprint Company
Post Office Box 2027
Toccoa, Georgia 30577
www.confederatereprint.com

Cover and Interior Design by
Magnolia Graphic Design
www.magnoliagraphicdesign.com

ISBN-13: 978-0692732571
ISBN-10: 0692732578

INTRODUCTION

The historical facts of this narrative were gleaned from published accounts of Mr. William Pittenger and other survivors of the Andrews' Raid and from personal interviews with Captain William A. Fuller, the leader of the pursuing party, Captain W. J. Whitsitt, of Ringgold, Ga., a Confederate officer who assisted in the pursuit, and other credible witnesses.

Care has been taken to record the facts accurately and impartially, and where the statements of the witnesses are at variance, preference has been given to the one in best position to know.

To the credit of the participants on both sides, it should be said there are very few discrepancies, and the gentlemen of the opposing factions seem disposed to accord to each other that large measure of praise which is due both to the Invaders and the Defenders.

To Major Hiram A. Butler, of Kennesaw (Big Shanty), Ga., for the past fifty-five years connected with the Western & Atlantic Railroad and now General Road Master of that line, the author is indebted for some heretofore unpublished incidents. Acknowledgment is also made to Major J.L. McCollum, of Atlanta, Ga., the present General Superintendent of the Western & Atlantic Railroad, for valuable assistance and for courtesies extended to the author in securing data and illustrations. Major McCollum was a member of the original Raccoon Roughs, organized by General John B. Gordon, and was at the close of the war a staff officer under that Chevalier of the Southern Army and typical American statesman.

Randell W. McBryde

Chattanooga, Tenn.,
        March 17, 1904.

Comrades all, of either army –
comrades are we all at last –
We who fought and we who suffered,
let us ponder on the past,
With all trace of hatred banished,
with all thought of strife removed
For the sake of these our brothers,
whom we honored, whom we loved.

Say not then that "I am Northern"
or that "I am of the South,"
Let the older ones forget it,
teach it not to happy Youth;
Let us rather, as the shadows
lengthen on our little span,
Glory only in the title
of the *true American.*

THE HISTORIC GENERAL

More than forty years have passed, and with them the bitterness of that strife which divided this great Nation.

Commencing with the generous words and magnanimous deeds of that great soldier, Ulysses S. Grant, seconded by the noble example of Robert E. Lee, great both in victory and defeat, and followed in time by such patriots as Grover Cleveland, Henry W. Grady, William McKinley and John B. Gordon, the gospel of peace and good will has been preached throughout the length and breadth of the land, until there is "no North, no South, no East, and no West," and the record of heroic deeds on both sides is read with pride as the common heritage of a re-united people.

The little old-fashioned engine *General* stands in the Union Depot at Chattanooga, a silent witness to the heroism of Americans of '62. You may, if you like, sit on the engineer's box and pull the same throttle that Knight pulled wide open at Big Shanty on the morning of April 12th, 1862, and you are strangely lacking in patriotic enthusiasm if you do not experience an accelerated surging of the American blood in your veins. Cold indeed is your heart if it does not beat quicker with the memory of the valor of your countrymen who manned this engine on that memorable race.

At the beginning of the war the *General* was one of the latest products of the Rogers Locomotive Works and was regarded as a fine type of strictly up-to-date locomotive. As an evidence that she was worthy of this name and reputation, it was claimed the distance of nine miles between Adairsville and Calhoun was covered in seven and one-half minutes in the famous race, a speed which compares favorably with that of engines of the present day and is the more remarkable when it is remembered that the track was in no way equal to the track of any first-class road of today.

In order to properly appreciate the high estimation in which such an engine was held in those days, the fact should be recalled that each engine was named and placed in charge of a regular engineer who soon became greatly attached to her and regarded her with positive affection. In this practical and progressive age, engines are regarded only as any other important piece of machinery – they are classified and numbered and made to work to their capacity by sending them out in turn as rapidly as possible, regardless of the engineers who must have rest, or in technical parlance, they are placed in the

The *General* – from a recent photograph taken near the base of Lookout Mountain.

"Chain Gang."

The capture of the *General* was one of the most thrilling episodes of that great war which divided the United States for four long, sad years.

Scout or spy, soldier or raider, call him what you will, James J. Andrews was a hero who will live in history as the man who conceived and undertook the most original and daring adventure within the enemy's lines during the war, and side by side with the name of Andrews will live the name and fame of William A. Fuller, the brave, resourceful and relentless pursuer who frustrated the great raider in one of the best planned and so far as it was possible, one of the best executed raids of history.

Both men suffered disappointment; Andrews died and won – Fuller lived and lost. Both men used their talents, their strength and their sublime courage to the limit of eudurance in the discharge of duty. Andrews "left his bones in Dixie" as he said he would unless success crowned his efforts and saw, as he had often wished, "what was on the other side of Jordan." Fuller lived to see a happy reunion of the Blue and the Gray and to congratulate the survivors, and comfort at least one widow who lived to battle with the world alone as the result of that famous raid for the capture of a locomotive and the destruction of an important railroad line.[1]

---

1. Reference is made to the Grand Army Reunion at Columbus, Ohio, 1889.

To understand clearly the importance and probable effect of the Andrews Raid, had it succeeded, it is necessary to consider the status of the war at that time and the position of the Confederate armies whose lines were invaded for a distance of about two hundred miles by this brave little body of men.

During the first year of the war, remarkable success had followed the armies of the Confederacy under General Robert E. Lee, which had the effect of arousing the North to a better realization of the magnitude of the task undertaken by the Federal army and at the same time of stimulating and encouraging the officers and soldiers of the Confederacy.

In the spring of 1862 the Confederate line of defense extended from Richmond, Virginia, to Corinth, Mississippi, the army at Richmond being under the command of General Joseph E. Johnston, and at Corinth under General G. T. Beauregard; the line of railroad running from Memphis to Richmond through Chattanooga, Knoxville and East Tennessee offered the only means of rapid transit between the two armies, and the Western & Atlantic Railroad running south from Chattanooga to Atlanta, and connecting with divergent lines to Charleston, savannah, Montgomery, Mobile and New Orleans was therefore of supreme importance to the Confederacy for the transportation of supplies and men.

The plan conceived by Captain Andrews and sanctioned by General O. M. Mitchell was to destroy several bridges of the old-fashioned wooden covered type, thereby cutting off communication between Chattanooga and the South, and leaving Chattanooga, which was at the time defended by a small force, probably three thousand men, under General Ledbetter, a comparatively easy prey to the Union Army.

James J. Andrews was a native of Hancock County, Virginia, but located in Flemingsburg, Kentucky, in the year 1859. He was a young man and was seeking a position as school teacher, but finding no opportunity for employment of this kind in Flemingsburg and liking the place and people, he began work as a house and ornamental painter in which he was said to be very skillful. He was also said to have had a beautiful voice and taught singing-school in the evenings; but, fate did not intend him for such a quiet, peaceful life and soon after the beginning of the war, he joined the Union forces as a scout. For this branch of military service he was singularly well equipped by nature; a fine specimen of physical manhood with quick perception, good judgment, diplomacy, coolness and unlimited courage.

The little company of twenty-one men who accompanied him on his dangerous mission were selected from various regiments and detailed to report to him for orders, but their services were not accepted until he had explained the character of the work to be undertaken, the dangers to be encountered, and an opportunity was given to each man to return to his company without dishonor, if he preferred to so.

They were all accepted by Andrews as volunteers to penetrate the enemy's lines in citizen's clothes, and Mr. Pittenger, one of the survivors, says Andrews told them explicitly if they were detected by the enemy while in disguise beyond the Federal lines, they would in all probability be hung as spies.

The plan and object of the raid was explained to them in detail at that memorable meeting in the woods near Shelbyville, Tenn., Monday night, April 7th, 1862. After this meeting, the men broke up into squads of three or four, and made their way through the Confederate lines to Marietta, Georgia, to meet Andrews by appointment and start on their return trip with the engine on Friday, April 11th. They were unable to reach Marietta at the time appointed however, and being one day late did not start back till Saturday morning, April 12th. This delay, as they afterward learned, was very unfortunate, as General Mitchell, who was to move on Huntsville, Alabama, on the same day, accomplished his purpose and the raiders encountered several obstacles in the way of extra freight trains moving south from Chattanooga with supplies.

The passenger train for Chattanooga left Atlanta at 6 a.m. and at Marietta, Captain Andrews and his party of nineteen men (two being accidentally left) got on board in groups of three or four with tickets to different destinations and scattered themselves through the train.

Hotel at Big Shanty, the breakfast station where the General was captured – destroyed in 1864 by the Union Army – Kennesaw Mountain in the distance.

There were three empty box cars next to the engine and ahead of the coaches, a fortunate circumstance on which the raiders had not counted, but which Andrews with his quick perception utilized.

Now came the beginning of the excitement. At Big Shanty only seven miles away, the train would stop for breakfast and the engine would be captured or the expedition would fail.

The name of this station was unique and the student of history will naturally regret the change to the more euphonious "Kennesaw" of the present time, because as "Big Shanty" it became famous. The name originated in the fact that at this point were located shanties for the construction force under Maj. H. A. Butler and being reached by a heavy grade the railroad men called it: first the "Big Grade to the Shanties" and finally, by an easy evolution, "Big Shanty Grade" and "Big Shanty."

There in sight of a Confederate camp, these twenty men from the Union Army were to seize the engine and make good their escape. Think of the odds against them, the desperate chances of life and death and the marvelous coolness and self-possession of Andrews, who was responsible and must answer for the success or failure of the great undertaking and the lives of nineteen brave men. None knew so well as he the risks to be run but his men knew the plan and could form a fair estimate of the danger. They scarcely hoped to escape without some resistance. They had reason to hope the plan would be executed so quickly in the absence of the train crew and passengers they could overcome such resistance as might be offered, but a single encounter, a single shot would arouse three thousand Confederates and even if they escaped with the engine, there would the loss of life and the fight begun one hundred and nine miles south of Chattanooga with the whole intervening country full of their enemies.

"Big Shanty! Twenty minutes for breakfast." Most of the passengers left the train, including Andrews and Knight, the engineer, the remainder of the party keeping their seats. Every member of the train crew went to breakfast, leaving the engine and train absolutely unprotected except for the presence of a few passengers. Now was the crucial time, the supreme moment.

Andrews quietly directed Knight to uncouple the train back of the empty freight cars, thus providing quarters for his company without disturbing or alarming the regular passengers, then with as much coolness and deliberation as if he were the regular conductor, though with the greatest promptness and dispatch, loaded his men in the cars, while he, with Knight, Wilson and Brown, mounted the engine and sped away without a struggle – all of this between the Confederate picket lines and in plain view of the camp of recruits.

One precaution was omitted; they failed to cut the bell cord, and when it snapped with the parting of the train the gong in the engine cab rang out loud and clear.

There was no telegraph office at Big Shanty

and Andrews knew it; the nearest telegraph station was Marietta and before a message could possibly be sent there the wires to Chattanooga would be cut.

They were off now in line spirits and with excellent prospects of success. Captain Andrews having posted himself as to schedules and meeting points, knew exactly what to expect in the ordinary course of business and trusted to his nerve and diplomacy to give a satisfactory account of himself and pass safely the several danger points ahead of them. They had barely left Big Shanty, however, when the *General*, which made such a brave start, commenced to run slower and slower and finally came to a full stop. This was, of course, discouraging and somewhat alarming, but the engineer found on inspection the trouble was due to dampers having been closed by the regular engineer at Big Shanty, and in his haste to get away he had neglected to open them. This only resulted in a very slight delay, which was utilized in obstructing the track and cutting the telegraph wires.

Andrews was now quite confident of success and for the first time indicated some excitement, in his enthusiasm going back to the box car where the men were, shaking hands with them and congratulating them on their successful start and bright prospect.

According to his calculations, there was only one train likely to give them trouble; that was the south bound local freight which he knew might be met at any point between Big Shanty and Kingston.

Tablet at Big Shanty (Kennesaw), Ga.

A red flag was placed in proper position on the train to indicate another section following, and to assist him in explanations which might be required of his running on the time of the passenger train. Being slightly ahead of time on account of their unceremonious departure from Big Shanty before waiting for the passengers to finish breakfast, they now traveled leisurely, not having the slightest fear of pursuit from that station and calculating that any pursuit which might be made, would be from Atlanta after report had been made from Marietta, seven miles south.

At Moon's Station they found some section men at work and secured tools for use in tearing up rails. The engineers were naturally inclined to try the speed of the *General*, but Andrews cautioned them to go slow, the schedule time being only about twenty-five miles per hour, the road being full of short curves and laid with light iron rails.[2]

They ran through Acworth and Allatoona and then stopped again to cut the wires and obstruct the track. There also for the first time they tore up one or more rails from the track with the aid of the tools they had captured at Moon's; this proved quite a difficult undertaking, but they had, as they thought, time to spare, and accomplished their purpose with-

2. Major Butler, Road Master of the Western & Atlantic Railroad, states the track was laid with 45 lb. iron rail at that time and there was no such thing as ballast. It is now laid with 80 lb. steel rail and ballasted with stone.

out being disturbed. The rails, so torn up, were carried away with them so as to make sure the track could not be quickly repaired, and this gave them a feeling of absolute security as to pursuit from the south. Stopping every now and then to cut wires, obstruct the track or tear up a rail, they at length reached Etowah, seventeen miles north of Big Shanty.

The traveler of today, crossing the Etowah River on a modern steel bridge may scarcely notice the small stream, so swiftly does it pass in the panorama of peach orchards and corn fields seen from the car window; but the mountain on the north side, rising abruptly almost from the river bank, pleases the eye of the lover of nature and if he is familiar with the story of the *General* he will notice a narrow, red line between the river and the mountain, which marks the track of an abandoned railroad. This was the private line of the Cooper Iron Works, and here, standing on a siding, Captain Andrews was surprised to see a locomotive under steam. This was the *Yonah* and Mr. Knight suggested that she be disabled and the long, wooden bridge over the river destroyed, but after some discussion, Captain Andrews decided this would be unnecessary and wishing to avoid giving any alarm or exciting suspicion so early in the race and so far from home, passed on. His plan was to burn the Oostanaula bridge at Resaca, thirty-six miles north and he had no fear of pursuit from the south on account of the track having been obstructed and torn up. This he afterwards learned was a fatal mistake.

Passing through Cartersville, just beyond, without stopping, they smiled at the surprised and disappointed passengers waiting at the station and proceeded to Cass, four miles north, where they stopped for wood. Here it became necessary for Captain Andrews to give an account of himself to William Russell, agent of the Railroad Company, which he did in a most skillful and satisfactory manner. He told him he had been sent by General Beauregard, who was in desperate straits for ammunition, to bring a train load of powder through to him at Corinth. Had it been necessary, he could no doubt have verified this statement by exhibiting passes issued by General Beauregard himself whom he had met some time before in Nashville and from whom passes had been secured as a southern blockade runner to bring goods from the north through the lines, but Mr. Russell did not appear to doubt his story in the least, the commanding appearance and self-possessed manners of Captain Andrews carrying conviction easily before him.

While the wood was being loaded, Captain Andrews conversed freely with Mr. Russell and asked him for a time card which was readily furnished. Mr. Russell remarking he would "send his shirt to Beauregard" if the latter wanted it.

Captain Andrews' feeling of security was now enhanced by the possession of an official time card of the road, which, upon inspection, showed Kingston, seven miles away, to the meeting point for the local freight they were expecting, and the confidence of the men was also strengthened by the cordial reception of the Beauregard story at Cass.

They reached Kingston ahead of schedule time and seeing at a glance the local freight had not arrived, Captain Andrews immediately ran his train past the station and ordered the switch tender to throw the switch and let them in on the side track, which was promptly done. This action, indicating a knowledge of the time card and railroad rules, undoubtedly saved him some embarrassing questions which might have given serious trouble.

So far everything had gone remarkably well with the Raiders and they had abundant reason to anticipate clear sailing for the rest of the way and the triumphant success of their undertaking, but "the best laid plans of mice and men gang aft aglee."

How about the men left at Big Shanty? Was nothing being done to stop them in their career? Fortunately for the Confederacy the passenger train pulled by the *General* from Atlanta that morning was in charge of a conductor who had rare qualities for meeting this extraordinary emergency, and when William A. Fuller heard the gong on his engine ring and saw through the window of the eating house, as he sat at breakfast, his engine and three cars disappearing, he immediately ran out and commenced pursuit on foot followed by Mr. Anthony Murphy, Master Mechanic of the Western & Atlantic Railroad, and Mr. Jeff Cain, engineer; Mr. Murphy having first dispatched William Kendrick on horse-

Capt. William A. Fuller
From a daguerreotype taken in 1860

back to Marietta to notify the Atlanta office by wire. However absurd the pursuit of a locomotive on foot may have appeared to the ordinary spectator, it was soon evident that Captain Fuller's prompt effort with the only means at hand, was not entirely due to impulse, but to a distinct plan of pursuit instantly conceived and executed. Neither he nor his comrades, however, knew at this time who had captured the engine, and did not imagine these men were Federal soldiers in disguise; the first idea being that the engine had been taken by some fugitive Southern soldiers who had deserted and were trying to escape.

Captain Fuller ran at the very limit of his speed for two and one-half miles to Moon's Station, where he met Jack Bond, section foreman, and a gang of men, from whom he learned the men who passed on the *General* numbered twenty-four or twenty-five: this was quite a surprise, as it had been reported at the station there were only four men, the remainder of the party having entered a box car without attracting any particular attention and concealed themselves. He was also informed these men had seized the tools of the section men, cut the telegraph wires and carried away about one hundred yards of the wire. This convinced him they were Union soldiers in disguise, or, quoting his own language, he "knew at once it was a Yankee trick," and fired his zeal to pursue and capture them.

So swiftly had he run that Mr. Murphy and Mr. Cain were considerably behind, and assisted by

Mr. Bond and two of his men he returned on a hand car to pick them up, resuming the chase under somewhat better conditions. It should be remembered this was not such a handcar or velocipede as is used by track men of the present day, but was propelled by poles or by hand. Two of the men ran on the ground and pushed the car while the others rode, taking turns at the pushing. Such a thing as a lever car was in those days a luxury undreamed of and the common practice of section men was to sit on the ends and propel the cars by kicking the ties.[3]

Captain Fuller now explained his plan, which was to push on as rapidly as possible and endeavor to reach Etowah before the *Yonah* left that station. They soon came to the break in the track and carried their car over.

At Acworth they secured double-barreled shotguns, but Captain Fuller says he did not have time all day to examine his to see whether or not it was loaded. Pressing on, they came in sight of Etowah, where, to their great delight, the *Yonah* was standing under steam, but at the same moment another break in the track which they failed to see in time, threw them all pell mell into the ditch. They were too much elated at the sight of the engine to pay much attention to so insignificant a catastrophe and picking up themselves and the car, they again

---

3. Major Butler, says he has kicked a car in this manner many a mile on this road.

got on the track and hurried on to Etowah. Here they secured the engine immediately, with a coal car attached, and took on six or eight Confederate soldiers who volunteered to assist in the chase. Captain Fuller states the distance of fourteen miles from Etowah to Kingston was run in fifteen minutes and he reached that station a few minutes after the departure of Captain Andrews and the *General.* Here to their great annoyance, they found several long freight trains standing on the main line which had been run past the station at the urgent demand of Captain Andrews to make way for his "train of powder for General Beauregard," and here again Captain Fuller displayed his wonderful quickness of perception and natural resourcefulness. Abandoning the *Yonah,* he ran again on foot, more than two miles to the north end of the town to a point where the Home Railroad intersected the Western & Atlantic. In this race he lost his volunteers but found the Rome engine as he had hoped, and renewed the pursuit, takng his stand on the pilot to look out for obstacles and give signals to the engineer.

At Kingston, Captain Andrews and his company were delayed one hour and five minutes, having had to wait for the arrival of three freight trains instead of one as he expected, the second and third sections being extra trains, carrying provisions out of Chattanooga, on account of the advance of General Mitchell to Huntsville the day before. Here also he was subjected to a great deal of questioning and his "Beauregard powder story" excited some incredulity on account of the movement of rolling stock and goods out of Chattanooga to the South. To this he responded, he did not believe the story of the capture of Huntsville by General Mitchell, who was not fool enough to run down there, but if he did, Beauregard was more than a match for him. At any rate," said he, "I have my orders."

As the delay increased and Andrews was more and more pressed, his men were warned to be ready to jump out on signal and fight if necessary; and weary of the long suspense shut up in the box-car, they would have welcomed an opportunity to fight, but the coolness and diplomacy of their leader prevailed and they finally made a safe start from Kingston, still confident of success. They had no idea they were being pursued, much less that their relentless pursuer was only four minutes behind them.

Soon after they left Kingston, they stopped to cut the telegraph wires again and place a few ob-structions on the track, and having done so, Captain Andrews, weary of the delay, gave orders to his en-gine crew, "push her, boys; push her!" This was welcome news to all, and they rushed on to Adairsville, ten miles north, where they were to meet two trains now over-due. It was considered neces-sary, however, in view of the several trains they had passed and the suspicions which had been aroused, to stop again and tear up a portion of track; here also they cut the wires and loaded up a large number of cross-ties, as well as other wood, to be used as fuel and for burning the Oostanaula bridge. While so engaged, they heard for the first time the faint but unmistakable sound of the whistle of a locomotive in pursuit; this, of course, made it more important than ever to make a break in the track which they finally succeeded in doing and carried off the rail with them.

Once more they were off with a full head of steam and going at a mad rate of speed, anxious to meet and pass the two trains at Adairsville as quickly as possible, and uneasy too, because of the suspicion of pursuit and uncertainty as to the character or numbers of their pursuers.

The men in the box-car were pitched from side to side very roughly, but found the rapid motion exhilarating and enjoyed the consciousness of lengthening the distance from their enemies and shortening the distance to their friends in Tennessee.

As they came in sight of the station at Adairsville, they rejoiced to find the freight train they had expected, standing on the siding, waiting for them. Stopping on the main line opposite the station and alongside of the freight train, Captain Andrews again had to run the gauntlet of questions in regard to his train and the regular passenger train whose schedule he was representing. Here also he heard news of General Mitchell's operations, some of the reports, as might be expected, being greatly exaggerated, but it was quite evident Chattanooga was panic stricken.

He learned from the conductor of the south-bound freight train that while the south-bound passenger train was scheduled to pass him at this station, the limit of time he was required to wait under the time card rules had expired and he had determined to pull out at once, leaving word for the passenger train to pass him at Kingston. This suited Andrews exactly, and he promptly expressed his approval and told the conductor Fuller would probably wait for him at Kingston, his idea evidently being to wreck the train where the rail had been lifted. Upon the conductor suggesting Andrews would of course remain at Adairsville until the arrival of the south-bound passenger train, he said explaining that the fate of Beauregard's army depended on his getting through quickly with the powder. This aroused the patriotism of the conductor who told him then to go ahead by all means but cautioned him to run very slow and flag around every curve to avoid collision. Andrews indicated his assent but immediately started for the nine mile run to Calhoun with instructions to his engineer to make the engine show her speed and rim as fast as possible.

In the mean time Captain Fuller left Kingston as described, on the pilot of the Rome engine, running as fast as possible wherever he found a clear track but continually on the outlook for obstructions and stopping every now and then to move cross-ties that had been thrown out by the raiders, until they came to the point where the rail had been lifted and carried away; which, of course, presented an impassable barrier, knowing the schedule of the road as he

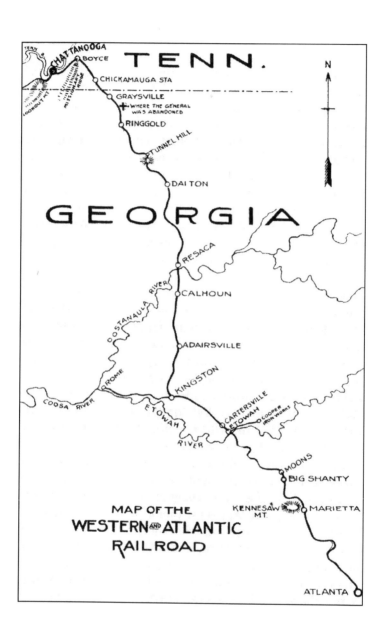

MAP OF THE
WESTERN AND ATLANTIC
RAIL ROAD

did, and recalling instantly the fact that a south-bound freight train was then due at Adairsville, four miles north, he lost no time in considering what was to be done, but unhesitatingly abandoned the Rome engine and called for volunteers for another foot-race. According to his own account, Mr. Anthony Murphy was the only man who joined him, and after a three-mile run over wet and slippery ground, they met the freight train, with twenty-one cars. As soon as the engineer saw them, he reversed his engine, being somewhat suspicious, after reflection, of the strange actions of Andrews and the extraordinary statement made by him at Adairsville, and scarcely waiting for explanations, the freight train was backed to Adairsville, the cars dropped on the siding, and the pursuit renewed.

Captain Fuller had taken his position on top of the head car as the train backed into Adairsville, and jumping off before they reached the switch, quickly threw it to the siding, then uncoupling the cars from the engine and throwing the switch back after they were safely on the siding, mounted the engine without coming to a stop. So quickly was this done the cars on the siding were still rolling when the engine passed them on the start for Calhoun.

They now had the *Texas*, a Danforth & Cooke engine, headed towards Atlanta and for the first time found it necessary to run backwards. It was also evident that Andrews, with the *General*, had gained considerably on them during the three-mile foot race.

Captain Fuller now had with him, besides Mr. Murphy, Peter J. Bracken, engineer, Fleming Cox, fireman; Alonzo Martin, wood-passer, and Henry Haney, acting brakeman, the four last being the crew of the *Texas*.

The race was now on in earnest. Fuller, of course, had learned of the movements of the raiders at each station he had passed and knew about how far they were ahead of him, while Andrews knew he was being closely pursued and was also in danger of a head-on collision with the south-bound passenger train, on whose time he was now running, taking desperate chances of reaching Calhoun before that train left. It was important for Fuller to over-take them as quickly as possible in order to prevent further destruction of track or the burning of bridges which would have barred his progress entirely. There was but one more engine on the road besides the *General* between him and Chattanooga, and if Andrews should succeed in tearing up the track or destroying a bridge north of this engine the race would be his. Both men evidently understood the situation thoroughly and the *General* and the *Texas* were made to run as fast as wheels would turn between Adairsville and Calhoun. Andrews now showed great anxiety and is said to have stood with his watch in his hand, urging his men to make the best speed possible. Engineers William Knight and W. W. Brown, and fireman J. A. Wilson responded bravely and loyally, and even the *General* seemed to be in sympathy with them and fairly flew over the track, leaping and bounding like a thing of life, and reeling from side to side as the rough places in the track were struck and safely passed. The men on the engine, of course, understood the dangers before and behind as much as Andrews did, though none of them knew who were their pursuers; they knew the desperate chances of life and death they were taking and enjoyed the excitement, but the men in the box car were not so well posted and to them the situation was most trying. They were tossed from side to side in the car, and while the door was sometimes opened for out look, they could only open it partially for fear of being pitched out head-long. It seemed the car would certainly leave the track and a terrible wreck was momentarily expected. Captain Andrews stated the run of nine miles to Calhoun was made in seven and a half minutes. Captain Fuller, following him on the *Texas*, states they ran nearly a mile a minute.

Coming in sight of Calhoun the crew of the *General*, running at this terrific rate of speed, saw the passenger train just starting to leave the station, but the engineer of that train, hearing their loud whistle and seeing them coming, quickly backed up north of the switch, which he threw and turned Andrews' train in on the siding. In backing up, however, he had fouled the north switch, making it impossible for Andrews' train to proceed until his train moved out of the way. The crew of the passenger train now demanded an explanation, evidently alarmed at the narrow escape they had made from a horrible collision. Andrews would not have stopped to explain except that he could not get away until the other train moved, and was of course in great danger on account of no wires having been cut between Adairsville and Calhoun, nor any obstructions having been placed on the track, but he calmly told the Beauregard powder story again. This conductor was not so ready as others to accept his explanation of the matter and could by no means be induced to start south to meet the north bound train at Adairsville; furthermore, he was in no hurry to move his train down far enough to clear the north switch and let this wild train out. Captain Andrews, however, was equal to the occasion, and after explaining the urgency of his orders to get through with the powder, made a positive demand that his train be let out, which was done. Here again a fight was narrowly averted, as had the conductor remained obstinate, it would have been necessary to use force to avoid delay.

Again they were off with no more trains to pass and the only thing to fear was the pursuing engine they had heard the first and only time between Kingston and Adairsville. It was only six miles to the Oostanaula bridge at Resaca and if they could succeed in destroying this bridge, the race would be won. Wires would be cut and other bridges burned, and from the news they had heard along the line as to the movements of General Mitchell and the condition of affairs in Chattanooga, the prospects seemed excellent of getting through to the Northern lines.

At Calhoun, Captain Fuller recognized a boy, whom he knew to be the telegraph operator from Dalton, who had come this far looking for the break in the wires, and slowing up as they passed the station, took him by the hand and lifted him into the tender. As they sped on their way he wrote a telegram to General Ledbetter at Chattanooga informing him of the capture of the *General*, and warning him to look out for the captors who were evidently Federals in disguise.

It was his intention to send this telegram from Dalton, twenty-two miles north, and he hoped to follow the *General* so closely as to prevent any further destruction of track or cutting of wires.

The train both Andrews and Fuller passed at Calhoun had as passengers Capt. W. J. Whitsitt, of the First Georgia Confederate Volunteers, who with ten armed soldiers, was returning to his command at Mobile, in charge of a number of recruits from Ringgold and vicinity. Suspicion being already aroused by the passing of Andrews, a brief explanation from Fuller sufficed to give the alarm, and Capt. Whitsitt with his ten regular soldiers, boarded the tender of the engine and followed the *Texas* closely in the race the remainder of the distance.

Andrews ran at a good rate of speed for about two and a half miles from Calhoun, when he stopped again to cut the wires and tear up a rail, so as to make sure of cutting off pursuit until they could destroy the Oostanaula bridge, now just ahead of them, according to the original plan. His men responded quickly and

South entrance to the tunnel.

North mouth of the tunnel.

cheerfully and Mr. Scott, who had all along been climbing the telegraph poles and cutting wires, was more agile than ever. Animated by an earnest desire for the success of their undertaking and stimulated by knowledge of the danger, they put forth their best efforts, knowing this would be the last work of the kind they would be called upon to do, for when once the Oostanaula bridge should be destroyed, further pursuit by rail from the south would be impossible, and they were confident no news had gone to Chattanooga as yet to betray them.

The crisis was now at hand; one more supreme effort and the victory would be won. Everything was soaking wet, however, and the burning of the bridge might be no easy matter, as in spite of the fact that it was an old wooden structure, it might require more time than they could spare. Here for the first time, according to accounts given by the survivors, Andrews showed real impatience; it seemed the rail would never come up. Tearing off his high hat and cape, he snatched a tool from the hands of the man who was wielding it and those who saw him said they had never before seen blows rained with such precision and force. Just then they heard the loud and clear whistle of the pursuing engine; it was evidently near and running at terrific speed; there was not a moment to lose – every nerve and muscle was strained to its utmost tension, but only one end of the rail was loosened; not another moment could be spared, so the loose end of the rail was propped up under a fence-rail, the men leaped into the car and with a bound that nearly threw them from their feet, the *General* was off again.

Now, for the first time, Capt. Fuller and his men were in sight; there were only seven in his party; Mr. Murphy, the four members of the crew of the *Texas*, and the operator picked up at Calhoun, but they were armed with guns and no doubt presented a formidable appearance as they dashed into view. Andrews' men of course were only armed with pistols and not prepared for a fight at long range. Fortunately for Capt. Fuller, the *Texas* mounted and pressed the displaced rail into position without leaving the track, for it was impossible for him to stop after this was observed and their escape from a wreck at this time was certainly marvelous. All hope of burning the bridge being now gone, Andrews' last hope was in some way to derail or disable the pursuing engine, and uncoupling his rear car and reversing the engine, he undertook to hurl the car as a projectile against the *Texas*. This was unsuccessful; as the *Texas* promptly slowed up, Capt. Fuller coupled to the car and continued the pursuit.

The raiders had loaded their fuel for burning the bridge in the last car and this was lost, but was now of no consequence as they would certainly not be able to accomplish their purpose. The cross-ties they had picked up were in the second car and they now punched out the rear end of this and commenced dropping ties on the track with the hope of derailing the *Texas*. According to Mr. Pittenger, these ties showed a perverse disposition to roll off the track and though enough remained to increase the caution and slacken the speed of their pursuers, the *Texas* was keeping uncomfortably close to them and for the first time the raiders began to feel despondent. Misfortune seemed to have followed them from the start. By diplomacy, courage, perseverance and hard work they had so far overcome every obstacle in their way and had repeatedly placed, as they hoped, insurmountable obstacles behind them, but their pursuers had been equally fearless, equally resourceful and were evidently tireless and relentless. Crossing the trestle, just south of the bridge, they dropped their second car, but unfortunately without, any attempt to derail it and it proved only a small obstacle to the pursuers.

Andrews has been criticised for not derailing this car, but it is well known to railroad men that while cars are frequently derailed from apparently trifling causes, it is no easy matter to derail one on a straight track without tools and without technical knowledge of such matters; and when it is remembered how closely he was being pursued by an armed party, whose numbers he did not know, there is no room for censure or reflection upon him for failure to take more precautions to insure success.

Passing through Resaca, the *Texas* was in hot pursuit, and dropping the two cars abandoned by the *General* on the side-track, the race was continued with only the light engine. The two engines were about evenly matched in size and capacity, and both were being run at the utmost speed of which they

A modern railroad — View looking north from the
tunnel — Village of Tunnel Hill in the distance.

were capable, the *Texas* being under slight disadvantage on account of running backwards and in constant danger of derailment from the ties which Andrews' men were still dropping on the track.

After passing Resaca, Andrews stopped long enough to cut the wires again, being uncertain as whether or not there was a telegraph office at that station, and, having no time to undertake the tearing up a rail, they took one they had previously lifted and loaded on the car next to the engine and placed it diagonally across the track, one end being under the rail on one side and the other on top the rail at the other side. Andrews evidently had strong hopes that this last obstacle would surely derail the pursuing engine and according to every rule and precedent, this should have been the result.

This section of the country is quite hilly and the road is full of curves. At each little stretch of straight track the *Texas* would come in sight only to disappear again as the *General* rounded the next hill and was hid behind the green foliage of the beautiful North Georgia forests.

Near Tilton, six miles north of Resaca, was a wood station called Greens, and here in dire necessity Andrews stopped for wood; hurriedly, almost frantically, working for their lives, a partial supply was secured and the track obstructed as much as possible so as to make a full stop necessary for their pursuers. Captain Fuller and the *Texas* seemed to have charmed lives; their pursuit was too rapid to stop, where just around a curve the rail was laid diagonally across the track, until, in some miraculous manner, the wheels of the tender mounted and passed over without derailment. They succeeded in stopping then, Captain Fuller pulled the rail off the track between the engine and tender and the race went on, only delayed now and again by the necessity of removing crossties.

Captain Fuller all this time was riding on the end of the tender and his wonderful skill in jumping down and removing the ties when necessary saved his engine and won the race.

Passing Tilton safely Andrews reached the tank a short distance north and was again compelled to stop for water. An explanation being necessary, the same old "powder story" was told, and notwithstanding the battered condition of the one car attached to the engine, it answered the purpose, and water was secured without resistance. While this was being done, a few of the men went back a short distance and obstructed the track, to insure another full stop of the *Texas* out of gun shot range.

Off again with water and wood and a good head of steam, they placed obstacles on the track at frequent intervals and selected a place to stop for a permanent break; again the wires were cut, and ties heaped on the track, while the remainder of the men set to work with all their might to tear up a rail. It was at this time one of the men suggested an attack on the pursuers from ambush, but while Andrews was considering the plan, again came the ominous sound of the whistle of the pursuing engine and both

Ringgold Depot – shelled from the heights
in the background during the war but not destroyed.
The stone walls are the same that stood then.

the effort to tear up the rail and the plan to attack their pursuers were abandoned and the race renewed. The fugitives and pursuers were now frequently in sight of each other, but never in range for the guns of that day. With the aid of additional obstacles on the track, Andrews managed to increase the distance from his pursuers sufficiently to gain time to get through the next station which was Dalton, and that being a junction point with numerous sidings, it was of course necessary to stop long enough to make sure switches were properly set. Here he made his explanations very briefly and escaped safely.

Captain Fuller reached Dalton a few minutes later and, thanks to the precaution of writing his telegram to General Ledbetter in advance and the efficiency of his boy operator, Edward Henderson, dispatched the message without delay – but not a moment, too soon, for as the last word was recorded and before Chattanooga had acknowledged it with the customary O. K., the wire went down, having been cut by the active and alert Scott about two miles north.

The *Texas* had only slowed up to drop the operator, Capt. Fuller understanding thoroughly the danger of the fugitives burning bridges and otherwise destroying the road between him and Chattanooga and pushing on with all possible speed. Andrews stopped, as it happened, quite near Col. Jesse Glenn's regiment of Confederate soldiers to cut wires and obstruct the track, but there was no time to seek a place of greater safety and they proceeded as usual in a desperate effort to lift a rail. They counted on their pursuer stopping at Dalton to send a message and hoped not only to intercept this message but to gain time while he stopped. Here again they failed to measure accurately the character of their enemy – they did not know Fuller. While they struggled with the rail, again the *Texas* was upon them and the race for life renewed. And such a race! Think of the best horse race you ever saw! Think of General Wallace's magnificent and realistic description of the Chariot Race of Ben Hur! Think of the strain and tension of muscle and nerve you have witnessed and I experienced in merely observing such contests for supremacy, and then imagine if you can how vastly greater must have been the excitement of participating in this race of locomotives with the fate of men and perhaps a nation, as the issue. Pulling and snorting, hissing and screaming, leaping and bounding, on the engines vent, the men heedless of danger, while fire and smoke belched forth and sparks flew from wheels and track. The fugitives looking back anxiously and watching the coming foe, while straining every nerve to increase their speed and racking their brains for some new expedient to hinder or destroy their pursuers. Success, reputation and, last and perhaps least of all, life, were the stakes.

Those in the rear looking forward with strained vision and exerting every energy to foil the daring enemy who for more than seventy miles had

Tablet near Ringgold.

evaded and escaped them. All thought of danger was gone – "Success" – the goal of human ambition was the paramount consideration. Andrews, intent on burning the first Chickamauga bridge, twelve miles north of Dalton, and Fuller determined to prevent him. Seven miles north of Dalton was a tunnel. Again Andrews' men thought of ambush, now apparently the last resource. What an ideal place for ambush! But no word came from the silent and anxious leader and on the *General* sped through the tunnel and past the little village of Tunnel Hill.

As the *Texas* approached the tunnel, Mr. Murphy called attention to the danger of ambush, but Fuller would not consent even to slacken speed and into that smoke-filled hole in the ground they plunged as into the bowels of the earth, reckless of what might be within or beyond it.

From the Southern standpoint, too much can not be said for the faithful and courageous engineer, Peter J. Bracken, who so ably and fearlessly supported Captain Fuller from Adairsville to the end of the race. The horrors of a wreck in a tunnel can be imagined and the men on the *Texas* well knew the danger of following so closely a desperate foe, who had all along been obstructing the track. The only explanation of their taking this fearful risk is that they, like Andrews and his brave men, were animated in the highest degree by that wonderful American patriotism which knows no fear. The light shone clear at the north end and Peter Bracken exclaimed, "Boys, we've got 'em now!"

And now came the last effort of the ill-fated Andrews. He ordered his one remaining car fired as they ran and the men obeyed with their usual zeal, using the last wood they had, with splinters torn from the walls of the car, to start the fire. This was slow work on account of everything being wet and some blazing torches were taken from the engine and over the tender. Finally the blaze started and the men crowded on to the tender. At the first Chickamauga bridge the *General* came to a full stop, cut loose, and left the remaining car to consume it. Oh, for a few minutes time! How anxiously they waited on the north side to watch the result of their last effort.

But here comes the inexorable Fuller again, and again the *General* flies. Coupling to the burning car, Fuller dropped it on the side-track at Ringgold, just beyond, and doggedly resumed the chase. At Ringgold the alarm is given to the local militia and hope is gone for the poor raiders. The ammunition of their fight was spent – without wood there could be no steam, and three miles beyond the race ended in the scattered flight of the fugitives on foot. Abandoning the *General*, she was reversed with the hope of wrecking herself and the *Texas*, but this, too, failed as the power of the grand old engine was spent, and the *Texas*, slowing up, quickly coupled to her and towed her back to Ringgold.

The command given by Captain Andrews was, Scatter in small parties and escape the best you can.

This was a great disappointment to the soldiers who had followed but so loyally to this moment and had all along hoped for an opportunity to fight.

Mr. Andrews, while not lacking in courage, had no military training, and was by nature more of a strategist than a soldier, while his followers were all men from the ranks enlisted to fight, and anxious to fight. These men were soldiers

> Millin' and drillin' and made for killin',
> Regular army men.

They scattered in various directions and some nearly reached the Federal lines, but all were captured, including the two left at Marietta; eight, including Andrews, were executed in Atlanta, eight escaped from prison and six were exchanged.

> The boasts of heraldry, the pomp of power,
> And all that beauty, all that wealth e'er gave,
> Await alike the inevitable hour,
> The paths of glory lead but to the grave.

CONCLUSION

The Andrews raid was great in its conception, great in the accuracy of prearranged details, and great in its execution in spite of failure in the results.

The plan was perfect, the selection of men as nearly perfect as possible, and the conduct of the affair admirable.

Every reasonable precaution was taken to insure success and emergencies unforeseen were met with rare judgment, tact and skill.

Not only did Captain Andrews command the expedition skillfully, but every man of his little company responded loyally and bravely at each step. There is not the slightest evidence in the testimony of any witness that courage failed or loyalty wavered in a single man during any of the varied trials of that perilous journey and marvelous race.

Post-bellum critics may find fault and wonder that certain, now obvious, precautions were not taken, but the greatest of human minds has its limitations and taking the conditions and circumstances

Monument in National Cemetery, Chattanooga, Tenn.

into consideration, the reader of this history who is fair can only marvel that so much was remembered and so little forgotten.

Failure was unquestionably due to the fact that on that 12th day of April, 1862, "Greek met Greek" – a brave American from Kentucky met a brave American from Georgia. It was the brain of Andrews against the brain of Fuller – the courage of Andrews against the courage of Fuller, and fortune favored the Georgian.

Two years later the victorious army of General Sherman passed south over the track of the *General* and retrieved the failure of the Andrews' Raid.

The *General* was under fire of the Federal batteries during the great battle of Kennesaw Mountain, June 27th, 1864, and was finally captured in Atlanta, where she was abandoned by the retreating army on account of some slight accident resulting in derailment in the Western & Atlantic yards in that city.

Other motive power and equipment of the road was moved further south at this time and the track behind them destroyed by Major H. A. Butler, who relates the final capture of the *General* as an interesting coincidence.

The Western & Atlantic Road was then, as now, the property of the State of Georgia, and the operating officials and men were regularly enlisted in the Confederate service and assigned to their respective duties subject to the military authority.

Major Butler says the engine was returned to

the State after the war in excellent condition, having been thoroughly overhauled in some Northern shop.

The *General* was on exhibition in Columbus, Ohio, at the Grand Army Reunion in September, 1889, and has also been at several expositions, including the World's Fair in 1893. The old engine is highly prized by the lessees of the Western and Atlantic Railroad, and is in charge of a custodian employed by the railroad company in the Union depot at Chattanooga, Tennessee.

By authority of the Congress of the United States, gold medals were presented to each of the survivors of the Andrews Raid, these being the first medals given to private soldiers in the war.

On a beautiful eastern slope in the National Cemetery at Chattanooga, by the side of the driveway and near a graceful weeping willow, the eight graves of Andrews and the other seven men who were executed in Atlanta, are placed in a semi-circle in front of a handsome monument erected by the State of Ohio in 1890. A bronze miniature of the engine *General* surmounts this monument and the front of the die bears this inscription: "Ohio's tribute to the Andrews Raiders, 1862, erected 1890."

On the left of the die are the names of those who were executed in Atlanta, June 18th, 1862, as follows:

James J. Andrews, Flemingsburg, Ky.
Marion A. Ross. Co. A. 2nd Ohio Vol. Inf.
George D. Wilson, Co. B, 2nd Ohio Vol. Inf.

Perry G. Shadrack, Co. K, 2nd Ohio Vol. Inf.
John W. Scott, Co. F, 21st Ohio Vol. Inf.
Samuel Slavens, Co. E, 33rd Ohio Vol. Inf.
Samuel Robertson, Co. G. 33rd Ohio Vol. Inf.
William H. Campbell, Salineville, Ohio.

On the right are the names of the eight who escaped from Atlanta, October 16th, 1862, as follows:

James A. Wilson, Co. C, 21st Ohio Vol. Inf.
Mark Wood, Co. C, 21st Ohio Vol. Inf.
J.R. Porter, Co. C, 21st Ohio Vol. Inf.
W.W. Brown, Co. F. 21st Ohio Vol. Inf.
William Knight, Co. E, 21st Ohio Vol. Inf.
D.A. Dorsey, Co. H, 33rd Ohio Vol. Inf.
Martin J. Hawkins, Co. A, 33rd Ohio Vol. Inf.
John Wollam, Co. C, 33rd Ohio Vol. Inf.

On the rear are the names of those exchanged from Libby Prison, March 18th, 1863, as follows:

William Pittenger, Co. G, 2nd Ohio Vol. Inf.
Jacob Parrott, Co. K, 33rd Ohio Vol. Inf.
William Reddick, Co. B. 33rd Ohio Vol. Inf.
Robert Buffum, Co. H, 21st Ohio Vol. Inf.
William Bensinger, Co. G, 21st Ohio Vol. Inf.
Elisha H. Mason, Co. K, 21st Ohio Vol. Inf.

This monument was unveiled May 30th, 1891, with appropriate ceremonies, including an eloquent oration by Hon. J.B. Foraker.

EPILOGUE

☆ ☆ ☆ ☆

War like surgery, is a painful and dangerous remedy for human ills, but oftentimes the most effective. This baptism of fire consecrated the sons and daughters of this great nation to the advancement of Christian civilization and the betterment of the condition of our fellow-men less fortunately situated, so that we have grown from "strength to strength."

"Instead of the thorn" has "come up the fir tree," and "instead of the brier" has "come up the myrtle tree." Let us hope we may with truth quote the remaining words of the Prophet Isaiah, "and it shall be to the Lord for a name, for an everlasting sign that shall not be cut off."

The fraternal ties so rudely severed in 1861 by the firing on Fort Sumter were cemented in the blood of brothers, and have grown stronger with the passing years until, in the words of that immortal American, Daniel Webster, the watch-word North and South, East and West is "Liberty and Union, now and forever, one and inseparable."

Captain William J. Whitsitt
1904

SKETCH OF
CAPT. W. J. WHITSITT

The early life of William J. Whitsitt was well calculated to prepare him for the hardships and privations of war, and this training, together with the blood of a heroic American ancestry, made of him the type of strong manhood he is today.

Any student of history and human nature who is privileged to sit by his spacious fireside in winter or on his broad verandah in summer, at his home in Ringgold, Ga., cannot but be entertained and charmed if he will persuade Captain Whitsitt to tell of his early life among the Cherokee Indians and of his wartime and subsequent life. In his retentive memory there is material for a dozen romances full of humorous and pathetic incidents, dramatic situations and tragic climaxes.

He was born in Orange County, North Carolina, October 7th, 1831, and came to North Georgia when three years old, with his father and mother, who were on their way to Mississippi but stopped in the Cherokee Indian Reservation, where his father died and was buried. His mother, a woman of strong character and remarkable intellect, remained with her children, her slaves and other property, cultivating at first the lands of friendly Indians, and finally acquired a large tract of her own by purchase, when the Indians were removed.

He enlisted at the outbreak of the war as a private in Company B, 1st Georgia Battalion, and soon rose to the rank of Captain in the First Confederate Georgia Regiment.

He has been honored by his fellow-citizens of Catoosa Comity with the offices of Sheriff, County Treasurer and Judge of the Inferior Court, and is universally respected within his sphere of influence.

SKETCH OF CAPTAIN
WILLIAM A. FULLER

William Allen Fuller was born in Henry County, Georgia, April 15th, 1836.

He traces his paternal ancestry to Gabriel Fuller, who was born in Scotland, 1709, and settled in South Carolina in 1740. His grandfather, John Fuller, served under General Washington in the Revolutionary war, and was in the battle of Camden under General Gates.

On his mother's side Captain Fuller is descended from the Allen family of Virginia, and related to Ethen Allen of Revolutionary war fame. He left his father's farm at the age of nineteen years and immediately entered the service of the Western & Atlantic Railroad, in which service he remained until many years after the war.

He was commissioned Captain in 1863 by Governor Joseph E. Brown in recognition of his services in defeating the objects of the Andrews Raid. After the war, he entered the mercantile business in

Atlanta, and retired a few years ago with a comfortable fortune. His hospitable home on Washington street, in Atlanta, is a favorite rendezvous for veterans of both sides, especially the survivors of the Andrews Raid, with whom he delights in rehearsing the thrilling incidents of that memorable event. The "sunset of life" finds him enjoying to an exceptional degree the fruits of his labors, and he well deserves the high esteem in which he is held by the citizens of Atlanta.

Capt. William A. Fuller
March, 1904

APPENDIX
The Great Locomotive Chase
Extract From the Atlanta
Southern Confederacy of April 15, 1862

Since our last issue we have obtained full particulars of the most thrilling railroad adventure that ever occurred on the American continent, as well as the mightiest and most important in its results, if successful, that has been conceived by the Lincoln government since the commencement of this war. Nothing on so grand a scale has been attempted, and nothing within the range of possibility could be conceived that would fall with such a tremendous, crushing force upon us as the accomplishment of the plans which were concocted and dependent upon the execution of the one whose history we now proceed to narrate.

Its reality – what was actually done – excels all the extravagant conceptions of the Arrowsmith hoax, which fiction created such a profound sensation in Europe.

To make the matter more complete and intelligible, we will take our readers over the same history of the case we related in our last, the main features of which are correct, but lacking in details which have since come to hand.

We will begin at the breakfast-table of the Big Shanty Hotel at Camp McDonald, where several regiments of soldiers are now encamped. The morning mail and passenger train had left here at four A.M. on last Saturday morning as usual, and had stopped there for breakfast. The conductor, William A. Fuller, the engineer, J. Cain, – both of this city, – and the passengers were at the table, when the eight men, having uncoupled the engine and three empty box-cars next to it from the passenger and baggage-cars, mounted the engine, pulled open the valve, put on all steam, and left conductor, engineer, passengers, spectators, and the soldiers in the camp hard by, all lost in amazement, and dumbfounded at the strange, startling, and daring act.

This unheard-of act was doubtless undertaken at that time and place upon the presumption that pursuit could not be made by an engine short of Kingston, some thirty miles above, or from this place; and by cutting down the telegraph wires as they proceeded the adventurers could calculate on at least three or four hours the start of any pursuit it was reasonable to expect. This was a legitimate conclusion, and but for the will, energy, and quick good judgment of Mr. Fuller and Mr. Cain, and Mr. Anthony Murphy, the intelligent and practical foreman of the wood department of the State Road shop, who accidentally went on the train from this place that morning, their calculations would have worked out as originally contemplated, and the results would have been obtained long ere this reaches the eyes of our readers, – the most terrible to us of any we can conceive as possible, and unequalled by anything attempted or conceived since this war commenced.

Now for the chase!

[The account, which fills a whole page of the paper, is omitted, as it differs in no essential particular from that given in the foregoing pages. In concluding, the editor gives his estimate of the purpose and magnitude of the expedition.]

We do not know what Governor Brown will do in this case, or what is his custom in such matters, but, if such a thing is admissible, we insist on Fuller and Murphy being promoted to the highest honors on the road, – if not by actually giving them the highest position, at least let them be promoted by *brevet*. Certainly their indomitable energy and quick correct judgment and decision in the many difficult contingencies connected with this unheard-of emergency has saved all the railroad bridges above Ringgold from being burned; the most daring scheme that this revolution has developed has been thwarted, and the tremendous results, which, if successful, can scarcely be imagined, much less described, have been averted. Had they succeeded in burning the bridges, the enemy at Huntsville would have occupied Chattanooga before Sunday night. Yesterday they would have been in Knoxville, and thus had possession of all East Tennessee. Our forces at Knoxville, Greeneville, and Cumberland Gap would ere this have been in the hands of the enemy. Lynchburg, Virginia, would have been moved upon at once. This would have given them possession of the valley of Virginia, and Stonewall Jackson would have been attacked in the rear. They would have had possession of the railroad leading to Charlottesville and Orange Court-house, as well as the South Side Railroad leading to Petersburg and Richmond. They might have been able to unite with McClellan's forces and attack Joe Johnston's army front and flank. It is not by any means improbable that our army in Virginia would have been defeated, captured, or driven out of the State this week.

Then reinforcements from all the eastern and southeastern portion of the country would have been cut off from Beauregard. The enemy have Huntsville now, and with all these designs accomplished his army would have been effectually flanked. The mind and heart shrink back appalled at the bare contemplation of the awful consequences which would have followed the success of this one act. When Fuller, Murphy, and Cain started from Big Shanty *on foot to catch that fugitive engine,* they were involuntarily laughed at by the crowd, serious as the matter was, – and to most observers it was indeed most ludicrous; but *that foot-race saved us,* and prevented the consummation of all these tremendous consequences.

We doubt if the victory of Manassas or Corinth were worth as much to us as the frustration of this grand *coup d'etat.* It is not by any means certain that the annihilation of Beauregard's whole army at Corinth would be so fatal a blow to us as would have been the burning of the bridges at that time and by these men.

When we learned by a private telegraph dispatch a few days ago that the Yankees had taken Huntsville, we attached no great importance to it. We regarded it merely as a dashing foray of a small party to destroy property, tear up the road, etc., *a la* Morgan. When an additional telegram announced the force there to be from seventeen to twenty thousand, we were inclined to doubt it, – though coming from a perfectly upright and honorable gentleman, who would not be likely to seize upon a wild report to send here to his friends. The coming to that point with a large force, where they would be flanked on either side by our army, we regarded as a most stupid and unmilitary act. We now understand it all. They were to move upon Chattanooga and Knoxville as soon as the bridges were burnt, and press on into Virginia as far as possible, and take all our forces in that State in the rear. It was all the deepest-laid scheme, and on the grandest scale, that ever emanated from the brains of any number of Yankees combined. It was one, also, that was entirely practicable for almost any day for the last year. There were but two miscalculations in the whole programme:

they did not expect men to start out afoot to pursue them, and they did not expect these pursuers on foot to find Major Cooper's old *Yonah* standing there already fired up. Their calculations on every other point were dead certainties.

This would have eclipsed anything Captain Morgan ever attempted. To think of a parcel of Federal soldiers – officers and privates – coming down into the heart of the Confederate States, – for they were here in Atlanta and at Marietta (some of them got on the train at Marietta that morning, and others were at Big Shanty); of playing such a serious game on the State road, which is under the control of our prompt, energetic, and sagacious governor, known as such all over America; to seize the passenger train on his road, right at Camp McDonald, where he has a number of Georgia regiments encamped, and run off with it; to burn the bridges on the same road, and go safely through to the Federal lines, – all this would have been a feather in the cap of the man or men who executed it.